# The Fantastic Adventures of Alex in the Broccoli Forest

## Paul Insel

### Illustrated by Richard Becker

California Institute of Human Nutrition Inc.

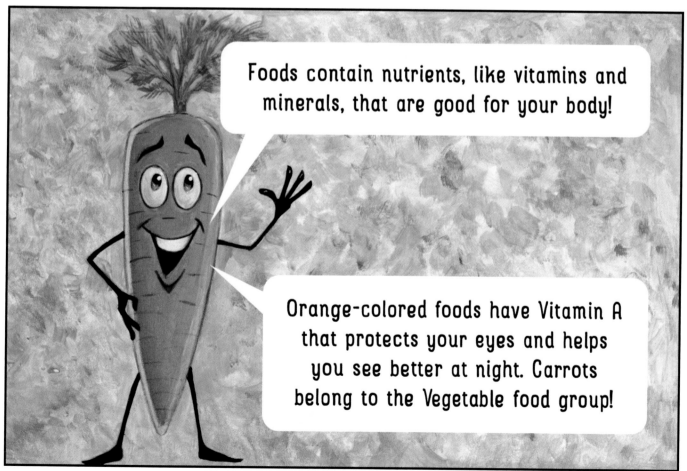

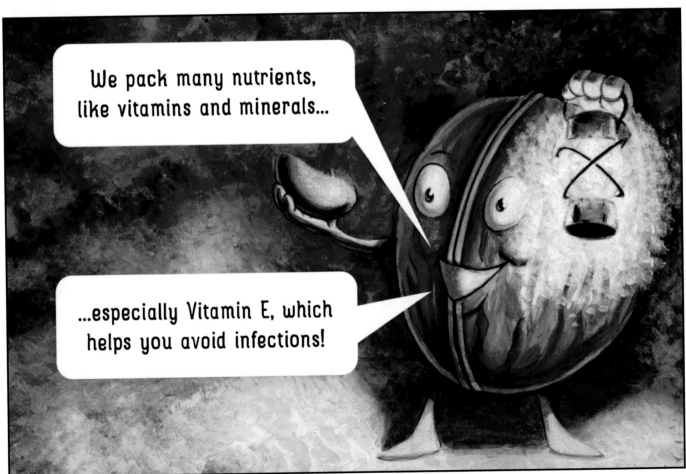

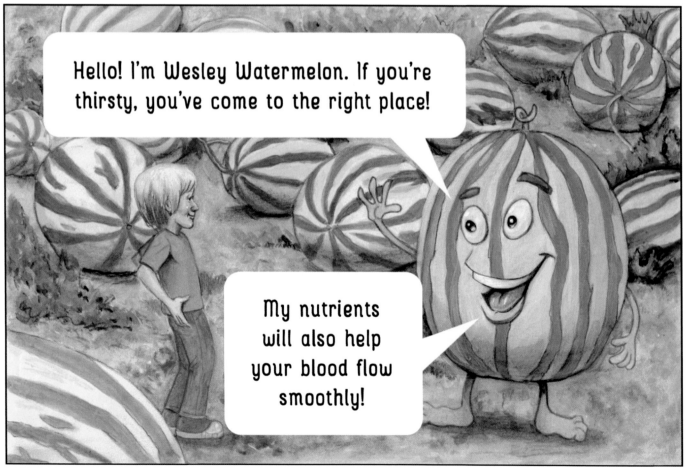

DAIRY

GRAINS

PROTEIN

# Puzzle Pages!

Can you match the foods to our food groups?

**1** Draw a square around the food that's from the Dairy group

**2** Draw a square around the food that belongs to the Fruits group

**3** Draw a circle around the food that's from the Vegetables group

**4** Draw a circle around the food that's from the Proteins group

**5** Draw a square around the food that is from the Grains group

**6** Draw a square around another food from the Fruits group

Take your time, and think before you ink!

34

**7** Draw a circle around the food that helps your eyes

**8** Draw a circle around the food that helps muscles work smoothly

**9** Draw a square around the food that helps build strong bones

**10** Draw a square around the food that keeps your muscles strong

**11** Draw a circle around the food that helps you avoid infections

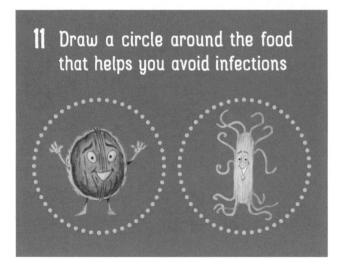

**12** Draw a circle around the food that gives you quick energy

Don't turn the page until you think you have the answers!

# Puzzle Answers

**1** Draw a square around the food that's from the Dairy group

**2** Draw a square around the food that belongs to the Fruits group

**3** Draw a circle around the food that's from the Vegetables group

**4** Draw a circle around the food that's from the Proteins group

**5** Draw a square around the food that is from the Grains group

**6** Draw a square around another food from the Fruits group

**7** Draw a circle around the food that helps your eyes

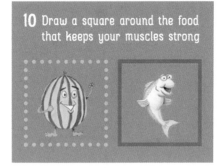

**8** Draw a circle around the food that helps muscles work smoothly

**9** Draw a square around the food that helps build strong bones

**10** Draw a square around the food that keeps your muscles strong

**11** Draw a circle around the food that helps you avoid infections

**12** Draw a circle around the food that gives you quick energy

How did you do? The top score is 12. Thanks for playing!

# Parents' Page

**Walnuts** are mostly made up of protein and polyunsaturated fat. They contain a high percentage of omega-3 fat, which has been shown to provide various health benefits such as helping a strong immune system response.

**Sourdough bread** involves fermentation which increases folate. In regular bread folate is added to the wheat flour. Mouth sores and fatigue can be caused by low folate stores. Pregnant women are encouraged to take folate to prevent neural tube defects in the fetus.

**Carrots** are rich in beta carotene, which your body converts into vitamin A. This nutrient promotes good vision and is important for growth, development, and immune function.

**Broccoli** is a super nutrient food that has more protein than most other vegetables. Multiple small studies have shown that eating cruciferous vegetables such as broccoli and cauliflower helps protect against certain types of cancer.

One ounce (about a slice) of Swiss **cheese** has eight grams of protein, which can provide ten to fifteen percent of your recommended daily protein. It also has substantial levels of calcium and phosphorus in it, so it's good for your bones.

Besides potassium, **bananas** are rich in anti-oxidants, vitamins and dietary fiber. They provide only 41 calories per 100 g, a negligible amount of fat and no cholesterol. Bananas are also low on the glycemic index (GI), which is a measure — from 0–100 — of how quickly foods increase blood sugar levels.

The bright red color of **watermelon** comes from lycopene, an antioxidant that may help decrease your risk of cancer and diabetes.

Enriched **pasta** is fortified with folic-acid — essential for women of child-bearing age. A serving of dry pasta supplies the equivalent of roughly 100 micrograms of folic acid, or 25% of the recommended daily intake.

One 3.5-ounce serving of **salmon** provides 22–25 grams of protein. Our bodies require protein to heal, protect bone health and prevent muscle loss.

The Fantastic Adventures Of Alex In The Broccoli Forest: A Children's Nutrition Story
Copyright © 2021 by Paul Insel
Illustrated by Richard Becker

Published in the United States by California Institute of Human Nutrition Inc., 702 Marshall St, Ste 619, Redwood City, CA 94063-1827

Library of Congress Cataloging-in-Publication Data is available upon request.

ISBN 979-8-54218-137-0

First Edition
10 9 8 7 6 5 4 3 2 1

Made in the USA
Coppell, TX
27 August 2021